the

wondrous

nature

of being

alive

praise for

the wondrous nature
of being alive

"Nature is a mirror of the human condition, and each poet in *The Wondrous Nature of Being Alive* has excavated a piece of themselves, reminding us of the grief and hope we simultaneously hold. These seeds—these word offerings—invite us to see, to behold, and to be renewed."

—Emily Barnett, Author of *Thread of Dreams*

"*The Wondrous Nature of Being Alive* is a delightful love letter to the Creator and His magnificent creation. Full of vivid imagery, profound metaphor, and universal emotion, this collection is bound to be a blessing to the soul in any season."

—Rachel Lawrence, Author of *Seashells and Other Souvenirs*

"Ranging from soaring and celebratory to winsome and heartwarming, and even brooding and introspective, this collection of poetry offers a moving reflection on all the spaces where life captures and holds our attention."

—David Lasley, Author of *The Hope We Risk*

the wondrous nature of being alive

Ali Noël • JJ Brinski
Molly McNamara Carter • Anne J. Hill
Rachael Watson • Ann Val • Rosa Gilbert
Kayla E. Green • Debbie Longstaff • Rynn Ely
Holly Ducarte • Vanessa E. Howard • Claire Hellar
Morgan J. Manns • Hannah Carter • Taylor Blayse
H. L. Davis • Kelly Hellmuth • Lara d'Entremont
Douglas Gates • Nathaniel Luscombe

For my wild and precious chickadees,
Scout, Boone and Clementine.
You have filled my life with wonder.

table of contents

creatures great & small

flora & fauna

introduction

Marcus Aurelius said, "When you arise in the morning, think of what a precious privilege it is to be alive—to breathe, to think, to enjoy, to love," and that is what the poets within this collection have set out to do. To acknowledge and confess that even if life shakes us with grief, trials, and tribulations, that being alive is a gift. In each season, in every fluttering petal or scampering shrew, there is an opportunity to marvel at the world around us and to see our place within it.

There is a time and place for everything under the sun. Wherever you find yourself in this beautiful—albeit broken —world, our hope is that you can fall in love once more with the wondrous nature of being alive.

—Ali Noël

1

weather & water

.lakeside.
JJ Brinski

Give thanks! For the
lake waves keeping
time, the diving tern,
the bathing breeze,
and this-here bench
for swaying.

HYDROHUSH

JJ Brinski

What is it about
the running river,
the rain, the
falls? Is it the succoring sound,
of motion and candied,
continuous drone?
Is it the cool feel,
caressing colder
rocks, pleasing to
the tired feet of the
traveler? Or is it possibly
the Savior's hearkening
yell over the water flowing,
of pitcher and pour,
over and over. The Spirit
he called Living and Water,
and it seems to be
the threshold, the presence,

the eternal insistence, the
very cycle perpetual—
cloud, shower, pool, rise,
rejuvenation everlong . . .

this tinkling thunder . . .

"the laugh rather than
the roar of heaven"

Mama, You Should Write About a Raincloud

Ali Noël

What can I say about these mighty sky drums?
Pouring their silvered honey to the ground
Calling life forth, washing us clean
Give me a thunder chorus!
I will dance, undignified
To the Maker's music
I will watch with wonder
At the rolling, growling skyward waves
Eagerly await the petrichor
Tell me, can you not see yourself in it?
This exploding burst of life
water, air and sound
Please – I want to live this way
Create in me, a raincloud

Golden State of Mind

Ali Noël

Did you know
I was born in the springtime
Near a city by the sea?

Perhaps that's why
I seek the depths
Dissatisfied with shallow dwellings

Perhaps that's why
I linger among the flowers
Content with happy, quiet things

They are, after all, so wise and unbothered
Here today and gone tomorrow

The King's Cloak

Holly Ducarte

You found me under a mantle of rain
In my melancholy, I sought your face
I needed to feel alive by soaking my head
To remind how you are living water
That cascades over as a rushing waterfall
Breaking away the roughness
Buffing off my view of who I am
I am not what the mudslingers say
The ones who think they know art
By splattering filth on a canvas
Without sense or beauty
Trying to form something out of death
Wanting me to keep donning filthy rags
No . . . I am made worthy in my cleansing
So let the rain keep falling
As I wear this cloak proudly
Knowing it first belonged to a King

Gentle Night

Holly Ducarte

The Night holds me hostage
In his lithe, willowy grasp
And sways me like the wind
As it enters my lungs, I gasp
Breathless and struck by awe
Of the moon through the trees
And the haunting call of a loon
Snaking its way between the leaves
I am beholden to the ripples on the lake
Mesmerized by its glittering glory
If I were as small to crawl
Upon mighty shelves of mushrooms
Could I say I was part of their story?
The Night will not give me up at all
He has no promise to let me go
As ivy vines crawl up my spine
My arms beseeching stars that glow
I dance with him, that shadowy gent
Becoming part of nature's tableau

Hailstorm

Vanessa E. Howard

A hailstorm blew in
Belligerent ice
Pummeling plants

But the sunflowers
In the backyard
These floral smiles
These badges of cheer
These light seekers
Stayed standing

Now in morning light
A bit bedraggled
A tad bungled
Leaves torn and
Petals missing

Their bright burn of yellow
Turns toward the sun

The Heartbeat of a Rainbow

Kayla E. Green

To lose what you never held breaks you
Dousing your sun with persistent gray
Rain makes you wonder if you'll get through
Sinking down in mud, feeling the grief never will abate.

They say hope is made of feathers
Further hope is weaved of love and light
As faith in what's promised keeps you tethered
Night turns to day and day follows the night.

The red of your loss stitches with more hues
And the seed of tomorrow burrows and grows
Until all the colors spread and suffuse
Now a miracle which Heaven composed.

For there was never anything so sweet
As to carry your own rainbow's heartbeat.

Tornado
Debbie Longstaff

Would you please stop growing, I ask as
I mark off another inch on your height chart
I've been trying to catch my breath
Since the very first second
My eyes alighted on your astounding frame

Like trying to catch a tornado in a jar
Or a supernova in a net
I cannot keep up with how
Your zest for life consumes the days
Like flame to tinder, or a hungry giant

You leave the house windswept and
Me dazzled, exhausted and breathless
But then I think of parents, like I,
Who do not mark that inch, just the
Days since the tornado's passing

I remember well the days spent with
Aching heart, cheeks wet, life forever changed
And I am suddenly grateful for that inch
With every fibre of my being and
Dare I ask, dear God, for more

Windsong

Ali Noël

When the winds unfurled over Zamboanga
Over a hundred years ago
Kissing my great-grandmother's orphaned cheeks
Did they know?
One day those eager winds would come for me
Teasing my melancholy, rattling the restless spirit
They gave to her, to me
As windsong swept through Wales' ancient hills
Along rugged Scottish firths and cobbled French towns
Whispering through Portuguese laurel
Did they keep the secrets of my ancestors?
Sung into the wind's minor keys
For this American woman
Who hears the song, their story
Who misses the world

Embrace

Morgan J. Manns

A reminder,
To find solace in the understanding
That every season bears its distinct essence.
Change, inevitable and vital.

There's a predictability
To the arrival of Spring,
A nod towards
Serene hope and new beginnings.

Drifting with outstretched arms
Through cultivated gardens and grassy plains,
Do I not embody the wild and free spirit of the petal,
Seeking to flourish amidst beauty?

As I mature, there's an undeniable allure
To the arrival of Summer,
Filling me with comforting warmth and wondrous delight.

A time to reaffirm
To myself,
To grow and to love,
Forever enveloped
In the sun's timeless embrace.

Then, as the earth tilts, so do I.
I embrace Autumn's arrival.
There's a savory quality
To the cooler days and muted hues,
Inviting calmness and harvesting healing.
For those carefully tended gardens,
Whose fruits now offer delightful sustenance,
The labor is celebrated
With earnest contentment.

And then, there's an undeniable charm
To the Winter's coziness,
Guiding me towards
Slumber and renewal.

It is time to rest, and I am ready.

In this perpetual cycle,
I find growth and reflection,
Embracing change,
In the dance of the seasons.

I remind myself to be present.

Floodplain
Claire Hellar

My soul is a floodplain.
It anchors itself to grief as though
It loves the water.
Tremendous Alabama storms roll through
Concrete city streets, and my soul drenches itself
In eagerness.

The cherry trees remember their own delights. They are quenched
With the bright pink blossoms of remembrance, gladness.
They hold fast to ardor, to the abundance of loam that circles their roots.
Trees remember better and older than humans do.
They recall that rain will always
Water this parched earth again.

Perhaps my mind, rather than being flattened by
Twin tornadoes of envy and depression,
Can find resurrection in all this reckoning.
In the immediate presence of grace.
More being-alive than anything else, as the way
Waterdrops sink below the earth to burst forth new life.

Fog

A Poem on Depression

H. L. Davis

A fog rolls in
Pale as bones
Silent as death
A sunken cloud
Coming to bring me low

My chest tightens
Can I flee?
But as the haze envelops me
Thoughts are dulled
Emotions, deadened
I am numb

I lie trapped, unfeeling
Not caring, not seeing
The mist a weight
I cannot shake

An empty companion
I cannot escape

But my hope
Does not depend on me
On what I feel
What I see
This blinding haze
Does not hide me from Him

For beyond this fog
Pale as bones
Silent as death—
Light still lives
And the risen Son holds me

My Winter Nights

Rachael Watson

This winter morn fog hides God's form
behind a misted hedge.
I want to find Him and ask why
life has this brittle edge.

I never asked for stormless days,
even clouds reflect light.
No, this concerns those darker things
that frost my limbs at night.

When I was young, learning to pray,
I spoke in hopeful lines.
It was spring, my faith blossoming,
climbing on lush green vines.

Now midnight prayers hold a bleakness
even dawn cannot break.
I've been plucked. I am buried deep.
I'm afraid, and I can't wake.

There must be a balm of minutes
that's God's answer of choice.
If softly spread, can time heal wounds
when applied by His voice?

I settle down beneath blankets,
tucking dreams in iced soil.
Hoping when this bitterness thaws,
He will ease my turmoil.

Cold Is the Bitter Night

Molly McNamara Carter

Cold is the wind that surrounds my soul.
Cold is the bitter night.

Deep is the cut the freeze creates,
deep within my heart.

My body shivers,
contracts,
and weeps.

Yearns for a winter sleep.

My soul cries out
its silent plea
into the space between.

Clouds invade the coveted space,
stealing the warmth above.

Absorbing hope.
Thieving away.
Hiding it in its grasp.

From far away,
the sunshine calls,
taunting me with its rays.

Daring me to desire it,
to crave it,
to invite it,
to seep into my bones,
through my skin,
through my flesh,
thawing the marrow inside.

Tugging my heart from the icy grasp,
allowing my soul to be free.

frost

Anne J. Hill

breath on icy wind
hear my tearless cry
frozen on mist
spilling from my throat
i can't
i can't
i can't

a whirlwind of frost
stilling my sorrow in place
time embraces the clouds
squeezing droplets free
i try
i try
i try

out of my body

get out! oh, stains of loss

melt and drip down white skies

splatter the rime with steam

i must

i must

i must

Shelf Ice . . . Lakeshore . . . Piled High
JJ Brinski

Yesterday,
I walked
on water . . .
jagged,
mayhemic.
Water,
frozen
in time,
unpredictable
underfoot,
and cloudy,
glassen-reflective,
a bulbous violet
tipped in cerulean.
Solid. Drifted.
Jutting.

Never will it be
the same ever.
But for now,
it bares
my footprints.

Fractals

Debbie Longstaff

Frozen fractals falling
From the wintry, laden sky
Each intricately woven flake
In icy flurries flies
The land beneath lies sleeping
The trees stand stark and bare
Each branch beautifully snow-kissed
The ground carpeted with care
Tho' the sap it has receded
When the days in length do grow
The world will start to wake again
New life will start to show

RIVERBANK REPRISE
JJ Brinski

At the riverbank
you will find me
in my sporadicosity,
intermittentancy,
on and off, off and on . . .
soaking up the consistent,
capturing call. Peaceful
streams can be running
things, ramping and rolling
over rock, trillion-trodden-smooth,
firm but mosstop soft.
It's the cheer that gets me,
the voices in applause and
chant, urging me to churn in,
leap feet-first, rush downstream
in anything but a hurry. Surely,
this is goodness and this is
mercy. Find me in the river,

learning constancy, fidelity.
Lord, land me in loyalty . . .
to this effortless flow.

Even Though it Hurts

Ali Noël

I float
Down the steady stream
of bittersweet release
The cord finally cut
Summer is here
Lush with promises
of starlit dancing
Laughing into the night
with the ones I love
Leaving heaviness behind
Running straight ahead
into all things new

HOPEBIRTHER
JJ Brinski

Hopebirther, bring forth.
Let light come down like
concentrated moonbeam.
Shine something today through
the mire and the murk
like lasers through leaves,
dark, dead shingles hanging
aloft on the branches over
this dwelling. Come heat and sear,
may unlikely joy erupt as a
house fire. Curdled flame
spill your warmth,
unfurling calm
in aromatic billows,
destroying nothing.

THE BETTERING BREEZE

JJ Brinski

There is a breeze that only
gains meaning at the end of
a long, heat-choked day. It
tucks you into twilight like a
mother's whisper and drowns
the noise of motorcars just
enough to call attention
to itself. By it, the day yawns
a fulfilling yawn. By it, burnt
skin is soothed with a
salve-smearing undertone.
Feet-up, pleasing breaths
inhale in triplicate,
transporting the scent
of new leaves, new neighbors,
and a new season.

creatures great & small

The Night Loon – A Haiku

Ali Noël

Like the mournful loon
Echoing across the night
We long to be known

A Fine Roost

Ann Val

I remember the first crow's lines
nesting on my mother's skin,
a small flock at forty.
I wished to shoo them away
drive their beating wings to flight so
I'd never lose her to the sky.

Found my own little flock
has landed at thirty-five.
Come, I say instead, build a fine nest here.
A laugh, frown, worry, squint
each a twig, pencil-width, precise—
woven through, over and under,
a life of lines.

Migrating Memories

Rachael Watson

Swallows return after winter's white pale,
settling on fences and on my home's frame.
Fresh air makes memories of her set sail,
coasting on currents of spring. Fewer came
this year. I searched the skies to no avail.
I listened for their trills, sweet songs so tame.
It seems most stayed with her beyond death's veil.
Soon, all I'll have earth-bound will be her name.
There's one bird that flits. Should I let it fly?
She may need its cheerful chirp more than I.

ALAS, A FIFTH
JJ Brinski

Baby jays and eastern blues,
sparrows, cardinals too,
and the woodpecker's working taps.
Four separate songs resulting in
anything but discord.

Alas a fifth,
vultures overhead,
signaling death
when my eyes strain to
reacquaint with life.

Screw those guys.

Reflections Upon Observing a Bumblebee

Kelly Hellmuth

Today I sit and behold a bumblebee.
He is bulbous and bear-like,
The beating of his wings
Reverberating in the chambers of country honeysuckle,
Filling the air with the deepest of thrums.

In my tiny corner of the world,
Country honeysuckle cascades and invades
Down towering cedars and cottonwoods,
All wild and uninhibited,
Perfuming the air with an intoxicating scent.

The gardener within me cries foul!
It's not natural! It's not native!
What about the sunflowers and the paintbrushes
And the purple poppy-mallows?
Will they have room to grow?

And yet the alluring sweetness of the flowers
Draws me in.

I sit on the grass in silence,
Noticing the bumblebee flit from bud to bud.
He does not make honey, I remind myself.
He exists on nectar, living a bee-ish life
Of uncommonality.

This is not the behavior of a normal bee,
I say aloud as I observe
The black and yellow pom-pom of an abdomen
Dance among the snow white flowers
That don't make sense among
Local flora and fauna.

How odd.

The wind catches in the trees,
The scent of honeysuckle swirling around me
And the bumblebee flies away.
I can't help but notice that
Both the bee and the honeysuckle
Disagree with convention.

I sit for a moment longer, contemplating
Things before me the world labels as invasive.
For I am a bumblebee, uncommon and distinct.
That which seems like it doesn't belong
Might be a sustaining, nourishing surprise
Placed in the way for my oh-so-uniquely
Created self.

I tell my inner gardener to let the country honeysuckle be.
The world needs more unconventionality.

To Gentle Souls: A Butterfly's Song

Taylor Blayse

Butterfly wings flutter earnestly,
A small speck of sunset colors against the
Vibrant shade of green leaves nestled in towering trees.

Gentle, delicate wings, yet
Strong enough to traverse the blue skies and land softly atop
Long-awaited petals.

And you, catching a glimmer of this quaint creature,
Relish in this flicker of a peaceful song
Written by nature; slowing your pace
As you pay mind to the small, simple things.

You are not too gentle.

With that softness that rests at the
Edges of your eyes, with those flower
Petals pressed along the lining of your heart, a soft spot.

Do not keep that gentle heart cocooned inside.

Let it burst forth,
Painting rose petals on the ends of your sleeves.
Let it sing a new, soft-spoken melody.

For the world would be lacking
Beauty
If those butterflies never woke and
Took flight; if they never trusted their soft wings.

You, too, can wear that gentle heart on your sleeve.

Let it brush gracefully against
Weary souls
It was created to meet.

Wings
Debbie Longstaff

My butterfly wings
Lie amongst broken things
Neglected and torn
Dusty and worn
Forgotten

Life's busy with cares
Necessities ensnare
'Tis love, not duty
Dirt and beauty
Fortitude

But one day I'll fly
In iridescent sky
Wings gifted anew
Dreams that prove true
Fulfillment

To Rest

Anne J. Hill

How the dog follows at my feet
Ready for every command or
Affectionate running of fingers through fur
No concern but for his master's will
Which has never led him astray
Oh, that I would rest so peacefully
At the foot of your throne
Head bowed and cradled on your lap
Not blind submission
But years of promises fulfilled
Through pain and tears
That you'll one day wipe away with a
"*Well done, my child.*"

who am i to question
Anne J. Hill

thunder voice from the fire
who grips the necks of beasts
crushes serpents beneath his feet
raw, calloused hands tearing scales
carving the bends of nature

lightning in his fingertips
roaring, depths, quaking

a glory long foretold
arms that snap dragon skulls
hair stronger than a thousand ropes
eyes that blind the sun
teeth to shred the demons' throats
a word to end all time

and yet, he fell

bruised hands that bled
a million sorrows on his head
to wrap his arms eternally
around the least of these

for someone like me:

who raised dragons and stirred winds
who conjured spirits on her sleeves
who fed the enemy and churned out lies
who bowed to the serpent's throne
and spilled out red wine on the rocks

this is who the dragon-crusher
holds between his nail driven hands
with a sweet anguished whisper of
my God, my God, it is finished

Let's Be Like the Fireflies – A Haiku

Ali Noël

Who follow the rain
Enchanting us with their dance
Little wings of light

Spider & Cicada
Kelly Hellmuth

Some of us labor with diligence throughout life
Intricately and resplendently steady
Weaving winsome works of art
Spinning away
Day after day
Forever willing to start
Our ravishing webs anew, always ready
To be persistently consistent through resistance and strife

And some of us wait
Obstinately brooding for seventeen years
Buried in dirt only to emerge as a swarm
Contentious and chaotic
Intent on making some sort of weird dramatic history
As we shed our collective skins
Leaving behind the Old
And proclaiming with our screams
An unignorable symphony of the New

To the Earthworm's Work

And to all the flowers you've grown without knowing it

Taylor Blayse

Uprooting weeds, taking mud and soil with me.
My purple glove a splash of lilac against the
Brown dirt and dull, damp greenery.

A place new color will be planted;
A place specially prepared for rebirth.
A soft space for my soul to land,
For my eyes to wander,
For my feet to feel the soft crevices of earth.

And in my glove, too, a wiggling thing,
Frantically searching for solitude deep within soil.
An earthworm, beginning his day's work.
A job too often disregarded.

Little does he know of his significance.
For if he were not toiling underneath the dirt—
Preparing and making it good—
My summer blooms would not shine as they do.
They would not be so daring, so bold.

Your hard work does not go unnoticed.

There are meadows of wildflowers planted into souls,
All because you were there, cultivating their soil
When they needed it most.

You may not always see the fruits of your labor,
The flowers you worked so hard to grow.
But I promise you, like the earthworm,
You leave beauty
Everywhere
You go.

The Songbird

Ali Noël

O, that my heart
would be a songbird
Faithfully singing out
into life's gray mornings
Catching hope
within its feathers

The Screech Owl and the Starling
Ali Noël

Did you know
European Starlings sing when they're afraid?
Sensing the danger of the Screech Owl
I saw one once, on a humid night in Kansas
O, I was young and simple then
Watching that tiny raptor trilling beyond my window
Eerie against the Starling's desperate song
I didn't understand what I heard that night
But now, I know all too well
Beloved, listen for the songbirds who call into the dark
Are they singing for pleasure, or plea?
Are they singing for dear life?
You cannot know
Unless you open the window

The Little Winged Bird
Lara d'Entremont

The little winged bird spread his wings to fly.
He wanted to see the world, fly through the cloud
Despite the facts, the fears, he was ready to try.
His toes left the nest,
Despite the wind's blows, he soars to his best.
But he loses control, doesn't know how,
Flying was harder than his confidence told.
He flutters his wings, but he's on his way down,
So he lays on the ground on his own.
The little winged bird who believed he could
Lay alone with only a broken bone to show.
The wind picks up, tosses him to the grass,
Where he now sits and waits, perhaps even thinks.
He must wait for his time, even if it's not today.
He waits in the rain, in the heat,
As he heals, he takes this time to sing.

He grows, he mends, he watches the wind,
How it rages and curls, it goes where it likes,
Not jumping too fast, but when his heart said,
He spread his wings.
Watch him fly, him glide,
Hear his song of sweet.
Learn from him
When you're tired and tried.

The Marbled Murrelet

Ali Noël

At the end of my life, O, Lord,
May it be some time from now
I don't want to lie
In a casket of *if onlys*

Did you know the Marbled Murrelet
Freshly hatched and eager-eyed
Will scamper its committed little legs
Through miles of dicey forest floor
Propelled by will and instinct
To find the moonlit sea?

If this plush little bird
So vulnerable and shaky
So creatively and beautifully made
Can seize the journey bravely

Certainly I
So beloved and protected
So fearfully and wonderfully made
Can venture across life's forest floor

Surely I can lift my pen
Again and again

Whip-poor-will's Song

Ali Noël

I've grown to appreciate the tenderness of Spring
With its vulnerable petals, its delicate soil
How like me, like any who have known
A harsh Winter

If we celebrate the blooming of tulips
Return of whip-poor-will's song
Night growing shorter
Why not rally, celebrate

A heart who breaks through the dirt of trials
Who blossoms up amidst the rains of heartache
Certainly you've noticed
How the sky cries too?

O, where would we be
If it didn't?

Communing with an Eastern Cottontail Rabbit

Rosa Gilbert

In the stillness I wonder
do we understand each other?
Creature to creature?
A branch breaks in the distance
under the weight of a robin's landing.
The almost silent snapping
snaps you out of our contemplative trance.
You turn,
my eyes met by a cotton tail
scurrying away.
Tiny hops vanish into the bush,
a curtain of greenery.
Gone,
leaving me to my thoughts.
I stay.

The breaking away
not enough to halt circling trains in my mind.
You skip forward, I am left behind.
Creature to creature,
our difference lies.

Farewell Little Fox
Rynn Ely

Your amber orange dances like
fire in the wind
Tips burnt black as smoke
Ebony socks stalking through the underbrush

I knew you once
an eternity ago
A friend
a familiar face

I'd found you
Abandoned
Alone
Afraid

I took you in
tended to you
held you
loved you

Released you
Now, I look upon you
like a stranger
under morning light

You've grown, aged
Bigger, now
Wiser

Your familiar coat, riddled in red
Your charcoal-lined eyes of gold
My little fox

Our eyes meet
the air stills
Do you recognize me?

I reach for you
but I halt
I cannot touch you

I can only look
admire
reminisce

So I sit in my window
watching you roam
Wanting, wishing
that you'd return

A kit emerges from the underbrush
and now I understand
why you'll never come back

I stay just a moment more
reminiscing on before

I know now
it's time to let you go
Just as you've let go of me

And so, I bid you farewell
as you disappear into the underbrush
from which you came

flora & fauna

OH VINETWINER

JJ Brinski

Oh Great God of Gardenscapes,
overfilled and flowing over,
spill out from your springtide
bottles of green. From your teeming
arsenal of art, flurry and drip
down mighty droplets of colors
profound, pouring forth.
Gush with superfluidity, rain
as I stand on this dead-as-a-dirt-clod
frozen patch.

Oh Vinetwiner, let the growing things
enwrap me, twist me happy all up,
spiral, dance in anti-death. Swirl.
Trumpet to life. Sing of bud and verdancy,
emerald veins, leaf-springing,
pastoral. I long to be utterly glutted,
skin-choked with growth.

Twiddle and twist, twirl about me,
a cocoon of exploded foliage.
A Dresser's hand commands,
new and fresh, wholly held
by life-soaked love itself,
in the fullness of richiosity,
thick, brimming, and round . . .
uparmored in floral array.

THE WHIRLYBIRD SEEDS

JJ Brinski

Helicopterous, you fluttered down
in one-winged delight, rested on
my shoulder. My upturned face
felt the sun and his care. With eyes
closed, the flying seed mingled
with my red-blond beard as I
wept morphing, maturing, gladsome
droplets. My face, the field. This
face-mane, the earth. This summer
seedwing, the hope for growth.
Numinous. Transcendent. Beauty
from new leaves, leaving winter in
the disappearing rear view. Hope
is on the wind, in the air,
felt anointing of tears on lips. I
pronounce one-lined poetry
in utterings of
angelspeak.

Daffodils

Ali Noël

O, that I could be a daffodil
Happy petals
Brightening dreary corners
Crowned mouth
Trilling Spring's ballad
Leaves outstretched
Awaiting shine or shower
Sanguine flower
Teach me, dearest daffodil
Ridibund warrior
Enduring Winter's frost

Peartree Buds – Haiku Stanzas

Rosa Gilbert

What are these buds, but
Poetry from the branches?
Sonnets to the earth

Of rebirth, beauty—
Even though they are not yet
Blossoming fully.

What are these buds, but
Closed petals opening up?
Uncurling gently,

A version of us.
Responding to light's soft touch.
Now everything blooms.

Like the Snapdragons
Rosa Gilbert

I remember snapdragons as a child,
admiring them when I traveled.
Wishing I could take them home,
plant them among the tropical flowers.
But they did not have visas or passports.
They were land-bound.

I am not.

I have flown to where they are and
made myself a home among them, instead.
Where his love and mine grew.
Where my womb sprouted.
Where she bloomed.

Here,
I have been planted
Like the snapdragons.

My Desert Flower

Rachael Watson

My daughter overwatered my plant.
Almost drowning it with her helpfulness.
This succulent once my sole confidante.
I hope its leaves don't lose their suppleness.
I find a washcloth on my bathroom sink,
dirty from when she wiped smeared face paint off.
Oh, here's a nail polish streak - bright pink -
and faint whiffs of acetone make me cough.
She begs me to jump on the trampoline.
Instead of cleaning the carnage, I go.
We disrupt the net's glittered dewy sheen,
our wild laughter in one mingled flow.
My child of the desert - she soars high.
Bringing hail and rain to my arid sky.

Brazen

Anne J. Hill

Little fingers covered in dirt
Pinching the trumpets and pulling
Free the honey
Sweet on my tongue
Summer's breath in a bush
A ritual longed for all winter
Sipping in the moment, grounded
Cares as sugary as the honeysuckle
How I long to go back to that youthful bliss
Toes wiggling in the mud
Laughter that spills unabashed
Heart beats cherished, present
Nothing need hold me back from
Discarding my shoes and running
Brazen to the nectar

Yew

Holly Ducarte

I beheld strong roots and limb
Wondering at your ornaments
Have they healed or harmed before?
I take a chance upon your beauty
As subtle leafy needles puncture
And toxins seeps into pore

My shame is hidden in your curtain
Been drinking the coffin of the vine
Ever closed within your shade
Tricked by an evergreen heart of staves
Science or lore, this taxus baccata?
O, the clever trap that Yew have made

Gone to Seed

Holly Ducarte

Life is frail
And I see it in the maple seed
The veins of youth
Feckless lines, shriveled
And yet . . . it still flies
Grows an entire tree
There is no less meaning
To the life it clung to
No less purpose
From the branch in which it grew
Yes, though life is frail
We know its worth only
When faced with its end
Mightn't we then collect
Every maple seed
And see them as a treasure
Like an old forgotten friend?

Hawthorn
Debbie Longstaff

It's funny how a smell can
Take you back to childhood
Sweet yet sharp
Woody yet floral

I passed it in a car park
But I was instantly 'home'
Amongst perfect white flowers
And many-lobed leaves
Brushing out my kitchen
With my friend's laughter
In my ear

Oh, to go back
To those lazy, hazy, carefree days
Where we played at chores
With no thought of tomorrow
Just tonight's tea

I realized that I survived
More than that – thrived
Even though I didn't worry
Between the thorns
I should listen
To Matthew more

With reference to Matthew 6:25

Leaves Fall
Douglas Gates

Leaves fall in the fall, which is convenient–
Adorn our ground with orange, yellow, red;
Tired of flapping, their trunks are lenient,
Permitting weak and dying ones to shed.

Impressed by death, our hearts attuned to strength,
This freckled earth is ringing in our eyes;
We think we've seen the height, and breadth, and length–
We've plumbed the depths, and reached into the skies.

The stalwart green impresses none all year,
Only children enjoy what always is;
Only they look up when the skies are clear,
All-repeating wonder, marked by stasis.

To have wild eyes, to be as any kid . . .
But like us, leaves grow old . . . and none forbid.

Not a Sound
Nathaniel Luscombe

in an empty forest a tree falls
and somewhere I sink
into the murky depths
of my mind
I've been cut at the roots
there's no one to hear me fall
no one to catch me
(what a long way down it is)
no matter how many times I grow
I always end up back on the ground
I am a living being surrounded by decay
the only comfort is that this death
inevitably feeds a regrowth
perhaps next time I'll stand longer.

I Swear It

Anne J. Hill

Write my lies on white coiled birch
Release them so they fold in on themselves
Hide from myself the truth of who I am
Camouflage my flaws in between the trunk rings
It's only a product of growing, shifting, breaking
I swear it

Paste leaves on my eyes, keep me in the dark
The constant whistling in the wind is normal
The rush of a thousand hummingbirds in my chest is right
The irritation in my veins, from Mother Earth
The tick, tick, tick of the maple-carved clock
That spins me around until I'm paralyzed is typical
I am not stuck
I swear it

See, look at all I can do in a day's work?
I've planted seeds and made whole trees grow before dusk
I've gathered leaves and traced their veins until they bleed
I've called forth whole armies of dryads to aid me in my work
I've pulled old oaks from their roots and thrown them to the sea
I've been focused and productive and I do this every day
I swear it

But then sun dips behind the tree line
And I lay my head on a bed made of unfinished dreams
The whisper of the night pleads with me, *stay awake*
And finish, finish, finish what I started
Forget the trees that grew and the armies by my side
For that one little leaf from many moons before
Is still slowly falling, drifting from above
Any moment it will land on my forehead
With the force of a fallen log
I'm a failure
I swear it

Tossing like the branches in the wind
I cannot slip away to dreamland
With bees buzzing in my skull
A hammer made of stone on my temple

Lists and chores and deadlines and and and
The call of the owl
The creaking of the forest
A cricket a mile away
Laughter over the hill
A spider on my arm
Breeze that tickles my nose
Turning and turning and turning
Focus on the humming of the river
Focus, focus, focus
But I cannot
I swear it

By some magic in the trees, I slip away at last
Here, under this canopy, I'm finally fast asleep until—
CHIRP. CHIRP. CHIRP.
Get up, get up, get up
But my body will not hear it
Move, move, move
The dryads beckon me, there's a whole day to be had

But it will not start until the very last second
When my limbs finally realize the urgency
Up, up, up

With heaviness behind my eyes, I stare at the birch I grew
All in yesterday's work, half a forest is before me
But today, I can scarcely breathe the same air
I swear it

I run my fingers down the paper bark
So much, so much to do
Water the trees
So simple and yet it's . . .
Walk to the river, don't forget the bucket
Bend down, fill it up, try not to sit in the process
Straighten back up, heave bucket
Walk, walk, walk
Don't sit down
Reach tree, empty bucket
Lean against tree
That was only one tree . . .
All the trees need watered and they all need done *now*
Feel the urge to cry but no tears come

Smack my palm on the trunk and pull my hair
Get the stress out, out, out
I'm not crazy
I swear it

Which tree . . . birch, oak, maple . . . I forgot the other trees
But they're there, lurking beneath my skin
Where do I go next?
And the dryads are calling
And the flowers are wilting
And the critters are crying
And the wind is whipping
And and and
I fall to the forest floor and cannot get up
I swear it

Breathing deeply, maybe it'll help
The grass bends from my breeze
Finally tears grace my cheeks
I shake in sobs. It's too much. Too much.
Watering trees shouldn't be too much . . .
Failure. Lazy. Selfish.

But yesterday I built half a forest
But yesterday
But yesterday
But yesterday
But *today* I need grace
I close my eyes and listen to the wind

One thing at a time, I tell my soul
And right now the thing is *nothing*
Sometimes that means a spiraling false rest
But today I've decided to stop lying
This isn't normal
I swear it

I reach out to the dryads and finally admit
I do not think I'm normal
They catch me in their arms
We've been telling you for years, they say
It's not an excuse, and it's not the end of the world
Relief and terror brushes over me
But the strongest note in the forest is
Hope, hope, hope
With ways to cope, to work with myself instead of against

Knowing some days, more than I'd like to admit,
Watering trees will feel like climbing a blistered rope to the sun
So I allow myself to rest today, even if that alone is a battle
Because there *is* hope
I swear it

Wilting Grass and Strong Weeds

Lara d'Entremont

In this dry summer heat
Like fallen autumn leaves
The grass crunches under our feet.
Though the flowerbeds wither,
And the water trickles into our wells,
The weeds push through acre upon acre.
Their green stems stand tall and strong,
Stretching toward the burning sun,
They thrive though the summer heat is long.
They cry, "Cursed! Cursed is this ground,
Because man could not deny the serpent's taunt."
Yet bright white wildflowers are all in bloom,
A beauty that still somehow thrives.
A reminder to the one grieving by the tomb:
Though sin's curse reins within and out,
Christ has broken its bind on you.

In the time in between we keep our eyes about

To watch for the autumn rain yet to fall,

The redemption to come and relieve every groan.

When the grass will glow like gold,

And sin's curse will never again cause us to moan.

Fear

Hannah Carter

The vine wraps around my neck
Strangling
Strangling
S t r a n g l i n g
It pulls me back
Unable to call for help
Unable to reach out
Thorns sink into my heart
The blood leaks
Words I cannot speak
You are not
loved
chosen
enough
The foliage grows thicker
As the vines draw me back
Ensnaring me

Does anyone see?
Does anyone care?
I have been taught to rely on the Prince
That only His Sword of Truth can sever these suffocating vines
So I wait, still and patient

Beyond the thick overgrowth the others talk
Of how the Prince came to rescue them
Of how He fights for them
And the thorns only grow
You are not
worthy
righteous
wanted
The darkness encroaches
As the vines obstruct my sight

Must I fight my way to Him
When I am so weary?
Must I try again
When my strength is sapped from fighting alone?

I am almost covered now
One with the overgrowth
When I hear a wearied voice inside
Nearly silenced by this lifelong fight
Do not
give up
surrender
die here

And I realize
When life means so much
When hope costs so little
This can't be the end
Strangled, buried, in fear
I want to live
To try
To break free of the vines
And strive
And one day hear the Prince
And believe
I am loved.

Moonflowers

Ali Noël

Sometimes I must remind myself
God did not curse the night
But blessed it with stars and haloed light
Established pale gardens to blossom in the dark

And yet, I insist on hiding my umbrous sides
My shadowy, veiled angles
But, surely, if he spun the nighttide
I needn't force myself to dance in golden air
Can I tell you how tired I am of trying?
So done with overcrowded spaces
I know daylight is essential
To rest, to bask, to grow
But night is for us, the moonflowers

When evening pulls its starry blanket across the sky
I bloom in the sacred quiet, this nocturnal soul of mine
Releasing my scented dreams, my moonlit praise
into the divine dusk

Snowdrops
Ali Noël

I like to believe
Snowdrops face the earth
Because dirt needs beauty too
To see it, to know there's more to life than
Rocks and worms, bugs and dogs passing by
Even if only for a short while
This hardy, solemn flower
Faces the snow, the mulchy ground
All too aware
The beauty of a surrendered stance
Draws onlookers in
Makes them wonder
If a flower bows in reverence
Why don't I?

Irises and the Souls Who Love Them

Ali Noël

It strikes the eye from afar
These tender flowers
Can you see it, in the strokes?
A hope he clung to
I know the feeling
O, Vincent

I wonder at the beauty
Born from pain
Purpled petals of gentle hope
To a mind desperate to know
A mind like mine
That it wasn't mad

THE SPRING THAT ISN'T YET

JJ Brinski

I will go to the woods,
for it does not argue with me
or seem to even have an opinion.
No, the woods seems confident
and cool, calm, non-foreboding.
Help me branches, and help me buds,
through another week of cold and
callousness, treebones, limbs in the surround.
My poor ears are beaten like the skin
of an old drum, my eyes need gaping
gulps of real colors and grounding
solids. Even this frozen dirt forces
firmness on my sore feet. And somewhere
near here, water runs as it always has,
faithful, rounding over rounded rock,
rushing, foamless and clear, to meet
the waves of the big lake,
thrown and heaved,
a force it cannot push back.

THE FACE OF THE STUMP

JJ Brinski

Jesus, Feller of Trees:
you renew both the face
of the year and the
face of the stump, letting
the worn cracklines of
weathersome oldness
bring forth scions
and shootlings like a
dry womb. Old skins
for the same new wine
like the blood of birth,
the thick oil of the
reborn. Crimson meets
huskless green come from
broken-open brown, ring-
featured and bearing a
slow-shaping grin through
yellowed teeth
clinging to dirt.

The Yew Tree
Ali Noël

Would I worry so if I stood before the yew tree?

Would life feel so urgent, so desperate

If I rested my hand on branches

The great-great-great-great grandfathers of my grandfather

Might have touched?

Would my sorrows haunt me so if I sat within the shade

Which has cooled the ground before Christ walked upon it?

I find it fitting, the paradoxical yew

Designed to save life, to take it

This ancient of the forest will outlive us all

Having seen the end of times

Time and time again

It knows its place in the story

What do we know of staying the course?

Listen for the Live Oaks

Ali Noël

If you want to learn the world's secrets
Listen for the Live Oaks
Seek out these grandmothers of the marsh
Cloaked in their Spanish Moss-y best
They will tell you all they know

I needed hope when the world shut down
So I walked among the Live Oaks
Beheld their mighty branches
Stretched to the sky in praise
And I knew, as they did, better days would come

If you want to understand your story
Stand beneath the Live Oaks
Consider their acorned ground
Marvel at their havened shade
Understand, your gifts will outlive you

acknowledgments

Thank you to the poets for digging deep, and to the people who support them. Thank you to our lovely typesetter and cover designer, Andrea Renae, for her stunning work. Thank you to Ali for editing and being the backbone of this project. Thank you to the beta readers who helped give feedback. Thank you to the Father who weaved creation into being and His glorious masterwork. We couldn't have done this without all of you.

-Anne J. Hill

about the poets

Ali Noël lives in the greater Seattle area with her three young kinds and rambunctious bulldog. If she's not writing or having a dance party, you can find her reading, baking or watching any take on a Jane Austen novel. Her work has been featured in Z Publishing House, SobreMesa Zine and Wow! Women on Fiction. You can find Ali and her poetry on Instagram @the.authoress.life.

JJ Brinski is a poet and flash-fictioner living in Marquette, Michigan in the wildly gorgeous Upper Peninsula on Lake Superior. He does life with his talented wife Grace and four growing daughters and writes in community with the Rabbit Room and Flash Fiction Magic. Having many passions, JJ spends most of his time loving space, theology, collecting typewriters, riding his bike ridiculous distances, making up words, and playfully arguing Star Wars. His lucky numbers are 4, 8, 15, 16, 23, & 42.

Anne J. Hill is an author who enjoys writing fantasy for all ages. Her love of words has led to her career as an editor and content writer. She runs Twenty Hills Publishing with the help of her circus performing best friend, Lara E. Madden. She spends her days dreaming up fantastical realms,  researching ways to get away with murder . . . for her books, arguing over commas at the kitchen table, talking out loud to the characters in her head, promising her housemate that she isn't, in fact, crazy, and rearranging her personal library—affectionately dubbed the "Book Dungeon."

Instagram @anne.j.hill.editing

www.annejhill.com

Hannah Carter loves to write dark, whimsical stories set in fantastical worlds. The main message that connects all her different stories is the idea that sometimes you have to fight for your hope—no matter how deep the darkness seems. She is the author of two novels—*The Depths of Atlantis* and *A Twist of Tides*—and one collection of short stories, *Saltwater Souls*, which are filled with mermaids, magic, and murder. In 2022, her story "A Home for Nova" won a Realm Award for flash fiction, and in 2024, she was a Realm Award finalist for her short story, "House of Shadows." In addition to fiction, Hannah also writes devotions, and has had close to two dozen published through various magazines, devotionals, and on her blog. The works of C.S. Lewis have had a profound effect on her, and she aspires to be both a theologian and fantasy author in the same vein as him. In her spare time, you can find Hannah either cuddling her cats, reading with a cup of tea, or listening to an absurd amount of Taylor Swift.

Rosa Gilbert is a stay-at-home mom and publishing assistant at Calla Press Publishing LLC. Born and raised in the Dominican Republic, Spanish is her first language. However, it was through learning English at a young age that she fell in love with words. She describes herself as a hope-filled poet and her work has been  published at Ekstasis, Clayjar Review, The Way Back to Ourselves, Prosetrics Literary Magazine, among others. She lives in suburban Ohio with her husband and daughter. You can find her writing at rosagilbert.substack.com and @rosagilbertpoetry.

Vanessa E. Howard writes primarily fantasy for young adult and middle grade. She has been a newspaper reporter, magazine writer, and college composition teacher. A member of the Flash Fiction Magic writing community and ACFW, she is also a homeschool mom and co-op teacher. She has been published by Spark and Havok and has upcoming publications with Twenty Hills, Quill and Flame, and Nightshade. Ms. Howard lives with her family in Central Texas. She can be found on Instagram as @writervanessa, Facebook as Vanessa E. Howard, and at her website vanessaehoward.com.

Lara d'Entremont is a wife, mother, and the author of *A Mother Held: Essays on Anxiety and Motherhood*. While the wildlings snore, she primarily writes—whether it be personal essays, creative nonfiction, or fantasy novels. She desires to weave the stories between faith and fiction, theology and praxis,  for women who feel as if these pieces of them are always at odds. Much of her writing is inspired by the forest and ocean surrounding her, and her little ones reminding her to stop and see it. You can find more of her writing at laradentremont.com.

Morgan J. Manns is a speculative fiction writer who believes the world needs more stories filled with magic and wonder. Captivated by the realm of intricate world-building since penning her first fantasy tale at the age of ten, she now ventures beneath the endless Canadian prairie sky with her supportive husband and two young children, all while eagerly contemplating her next literary creation. While her current occupation is that of an elementary school teacher, her dream job will always be dragon rider, soaring through the skies of her imaginings.

Taylor Blayse is a wife, writer, and greenhouse manager for her family's business, The Garden Party. She holds a B.A. in both music and English from the University of Missouri. In her writing, Taylor loves to explore themes of hope, whimsy, wonder, and childlike faith. Her writing has been published at Calla Press, The

Way Back to Ourselves, Prosetrics, among others. When she isn't writing, she can be found reading, spending time with friends, gardening, wandering around bookstores, and enjoying the outdoors. To read more of her poetry, visit her substack: @taylorblayse or her instagram: @taylorblayse.

 Kelly Hellmuth loves to tell compelling stories to kids of all ages. She originally began crafting worlds for her own children and is currently working on her first novel. Kelly has been published in Havok and Twenty Hills anthologies and has upcoming publications with Dragon Bone Press. More of Kelly's writing can be found on Instagram at @khelmetauthor, where she regularly writes flash fiction and poetry with a wonderful cottage full of creative souls. When Kelly isn't writing, she teaches high school literature and Latin and dabbles in a variety of artistic pursuits.

Molly McNamara Carter has been writing stories since she learned to read them. Born in upstate New York, she has lived in two countries and six US states. She has a BA in English, loves reading, writing, traveling, being outside and exploring new places with her favorite people. She is the  author of several books for young people and select pieces of poetry. She currently lives in Arizona with her husband, three children, and never enough books. You can find out more about Molly and her work at www.mollymcnamaracarter.com.

H. L. Davis is a Christian, wife, and homeschool mom who calls the South home. She has written and published multiple short stories both in print and online, primarily with Havok Publishing and Twenty Hills. When she isn't brainstorming ideas and weaving words into stories, she enjoys reading, graphic design, and quality time with her family and friends. You can find her on Instagram @h.l.davis_stories or on her Substack, hldavisstories.substack.com.

Nathaniel Luscombe is an author and publisher from Ontario, Canada. He's known for his existential writing, fun mashups of speculative genres, and making everything cozy (even horror). His most popular work is his science-fantasy novella *Moon Soul*. When he's  not writing, he's busy co-running Dragon Bone Publishing and Dragon Heart Press.

Ann Val earns a living writing for adults, but it's telling stories to children that she finds most endearing. She is a wife and mother of three editors-in-training. Her work appears in several forthcoming anthologies with Twenty Hills, and her picture book, *La Banana*, was published by Middle Creek Publishing. Find her online at @annvalwrites and on Substack as "The Guide Girl."

Douglas Gates is a lawn care professional living and working in his hometown of Boise, Idaho. Shooting the breeze in the work truck helps him to flesh out his ideas and thoughts on things, which he proceeds to record in sonnet form. He also runs a nonprofit which assists in caring for a particular group of vulnerable  children in Uganda. To unwind, he practices at-home yoga and keeps up with the local art scene. His writing influences include GK Chesterton and Alexander Pope.

Holly Ducarte is a creative writer and a two-time award-winning poet from Alberta, Canada. She currently resides in a modest lake town with her husband, daughter, and two cats. Her publications include two poetry collections titled *Moths, Rust & The Things That Stay* and *Confetti Confessions*, a YA novel titled *The Light Over Broken Tide*, and several short stories, one of which was nominated for an award in literature. She is an old soul that enjoys reading good books, going on nature walks, shopping in antique stores, watercolor painting, junk-journaling, visits with family and friends, binging fave movies and tv shows, shameless dancing, listening to a variety of music, Instagramming, good food with tea and coffee, and growing in the Christian faith.

Kayla E. Green is an author and poet who writes to remind others—and herself—that light always prevails over darkness. When she isn't writing, reading, or spending time with her family, she loves singing loudly and off-key to KLove Radio and pretending she's a unicorn. She has written an award-  winning YA fantasy novella, *Aivan: The One Truth*, and an inspirational poetry collection, *Metamorphosis*. Kayla also has stories and poems featured in various anthologies as well as contest-winning stories published in Clean Fiction Magazine and online with WOW! Women on Writing. Additionally, she has several flash fiction stories available through Havok Publishing. Kayla's next YA fantasy novel is set to debut in 2025. Learn more and connect with her at theunicornwriter.com and on Instagram @theunicornwriter93.

Born near London, Debbie Longstaff now lives in the English countryside in a fixer-upper with her large and wonderful neurodiverse family and cuddly labradors. Whilst running several businesses with her extremely hardworking husband she recently fulfilled a long-held dream and graduated with a Masters degree in Creative Writing. When not gardening, looking for fossils on the Jurassic Coast or stargazing through her son's telescope, Debbie can be found writing poetry, buying and reading far too many books, drinking tea and entering writing competitions. She is also working very hard on her timey-wimey Middle Grade sci fi fantasy series, which she hopes to publish one day. And then, just maybe, she'll be able to finish her house and study for the PhD she longs for. Debbie can be found on Instagram at: @debbielongstaffauthor.

Claire Hellar grew up as a missionary kid in Papua New Guinea and her travels eventually landed her in Birmingham Alabama. She works in marketing and loves peonies, Tolstoy, mountains, and prayer.

 Rachael Watson is completing an Undergraduate Diploma in Creative Writing at the University of Oxford. Several of her short stories have been published online and in print. Rachael enjoys writing fiction across multiple genres, from thriller to fantasy to middle grade, pulling on the imaginative strings of "What if?" to see where the unraveling takes her. Inspired by her previous career in dance performance and choreography, she aims to create stories that have an effortless flow. You can find Rachael on Instagram as @rachaelwithastory.

Rynn Ely emerges as a fresh voice in the literary world. While her pen has long been busy, it was only recently that she turned her aspirations of becoming an author into reality. Having earned an Undergraduate degree in Criminal Justice with minors in Sociology and Literature in 2021, Rynn finally decided to  take the plunge and dedicate her time to cultivating her passion. When not writing and working her day-job, Rynn can be found cuddled up with her partner, two dogs, and two cats, or traversing the globe in search of new adventures.

www.annejhill.com/twenty-hills-publishing

Instagram @twenty_hills